THE LIVING GOSPEL

Daily Devotions for Lent 2013

R. Scott Hurd

ave maria press notre dame, indiana

© 2012 by R. Scott Hurd

Founded in 1865, Ave Maria Press is a ministry of the United States
Province of Holy Cross.

www.avemariapress.com

Paperback: ISBN-10 1-59471-363-4, ISBN-13 978-1-59471-363-7

Cover image "At the Foot of the Cross" ©2012 by Jeni Butler,
artworkbyjeni.wix.com

Cover design by John Carson.

Text design by Kathy Coleman.

Printed and bound in the United States of America.

INTRODUCTION

Flames typically turn what they touch into ashes. Quite an opposite dynamic, however, happens during the season of Lent. We begin with ashes solemnly traced on our foreheads on Ash Wednesday, and we end with vibrant flames of the new Easter fire at the beginning of the Vigil on Holy Saturday night. As the ashes called us to repent, the flames call us to the resurrected Christ, our true and only light.

Lent, then, might be understood as a yearly journey from ashes to living flame, from death to new life. Should we choose to make this journey, we'll discover it to be a rich opportunity for spiritual growth, renewal, and continued conversion by opening ourselves more fully to grace, listening more attentively to the Word of God, and extending ourselves in compassionate service to others.

We foster this Lenten process through discipline. We "give something up" or "take something on." This little book can be a useful part of your Lenten discipline and a helpful companion on your journey. It includes a brief devotion for every day from Ash Wednesday through Good Friday. Each two-page devotion features an invitation to enter into silence to listen for God's voice; a prayer to place you consciously in God's presence and open yourself to grace; a selection from the Gospel reading appointed for Mass that day; a brief meditation to help break open God's Word; and a suggested action step to help translate devotion into deed and solitude into service.

To benefit the most from this book, try to pray each devotion on its appointed day. You can do this at any time: with a morning cup of coffee, during lunch break at your desk, before or after daily Mass, or in bed before you turn out the light. Depending on your schedule or commitments, you can choose to spend as much or as little time with each chapter as you wish. However, at least five minutes a day is a good starting point. You may use a bible along with this booklet if you want to read the entire gospel reading for the day and not just the verses printed in this booklet. However, time may be tight on many days and at those times focus on what you are able.

It is my prayer that this book will be a blessing to you, allow God to touch your heart, help you observe a good and holy Lent, inspire you to generous service, and transform your life from ashes into living flame.

> May the light of Christ rising in glory
> dispel the darkness of our hearts and minds.
>
> ~*Easter Vigil Liturgy*

Brothers and sisters:
We are ambassadors for Christ,
as if God were appealing through us.
We implore you on behalf of Christ,
be reconciled to God.

~2 Corinthians 5:20

Ash Wednesday

BEGIN

Spend a minute or two in silence. Set aside whatever might hinder your prayer.

PRAY

If today you hear his voice, harden not your hearts.

~Psalm 95:7–8

LISTEN

Read Matthew 6:1-6, 16-18

Jesus said to his disciples:
"Take care not to perform righteous deeds in order that people may see them; otherwise, you will have no recompense from your heavenly Father."

~Matthew 6:1

Serving in Secret

"Bad publicity is better than no publicity." This catch-phrase betrays a deep desire within so many of us to "see and be seen"—no matter the reason or the cost. We love attention, to be noticed, affirmed, and especially praised. That's why the words of Jesus in the gospel reading today are so challenging.

Jesus tells us to guard against performing religious acts for others to see. Our left hand must not know what our right hand is doing; we're to pray in private behind closed doors; and our appearance shouldn't reveal that we're fasting.

Jesus knows that we often bring mixed motives to our religious undertakings. Some of our motivations—the ones inspired by God—are noble and good, like wanting to serve others, help the poor, work for justice, alleviate suffering, grow closer to God, and make amends for our sins. But sometimes we have other motives that aren't as laudable. We may do religious things because we hope others will see us as holy, or at least good, and perhaps admire us for the kind things we've done.

When we act in this way, we're seeking to glorify ourselves—and there's the catch. As Christians, all we do, in one way or another, should be done for the glory of God. As we journey through the days of Lent, let's ask the Lord to purify our motives, so that what we do is not driven by concern for public relations, but by a genuine spirit of praise and humble commitment to the Gospel.

ACT

I will write down my Lenten resolutions, specifying how I intend to fast, pray, and help the poor this year as I prepare for Easter.

PRAY

Lord God, help me find a place of solitude this Lent where I can lay down my burdens and find freedom from my sins. Amen.

Thursday after Ash Wednesday

Spend a minute or two in silence. Set aside whatever might hinder your prayer.

PRAY

Repent, says the Lord; the kingdom of heaven is at hand.

~Matthew 4:17

LISTEN

Read Luke 9:22–25

Then he said to all,
"If anyone wishes to come after me, he must deny himself and take up his cross daily and follow me."

~Luke 9:23

Our Proper Direction

An old joke asks: Why did Moses and the Israelites wander in the wilderness for forty years? Because they didn't ask for directions! Like the Israelites, we are on a journey toward freedom—not of forty years, but of forty days. And good directions are just as important for us. Consider the directions we can find in today's gospel reading. Jesus invites us to carry crosses on our journey—crosses that are the inevitable hardships and sufferings of any human life. Jesus stresses, however, that when we carry a cross, we are to follow him. That's our proper direction.

If we take off in a different direction with our crosses, and follow a path different from our Lord's, we'll likely wind up exhausted, resentful, alone, even despairing. Chances are we won't get very far, because our cross will have become too heavy to bear.

But when we follow Jesus, we'll be given the courage that we need to carry on, and a strength that can only come as God's gift. We'll have the consolation of seeing Jesus' footsteps before us, or even planted right alongside ours. And we'll be assured that our journey isn't pointless, because it has the promise of a perfect destination—an eternity of rest and peace with him.

Carrying the crosses life inevitably brings is the hardest part of our journey in faith. But our Lord knows that, because he carried one too. That's why he doesn't want us to carry *our* crosses alone.

ACT

I will identify the heaviest cross I am carrying right now. It may be illness, unemployment, a difficult or broken relationship, a child in trouble, frustration at work, or any number of other struggles. As I name that burden I will imagine that I hold it in my hands, offering it to Jesus as I pray.

PRAY

Jesus crucified, walk with me as I bear this cross. Let me not abandon my struggle, but help me with the spirit-crushing weight of it. I open my hands and my heart to your redeeming love. Amen.

FRIDAY AFTER ASH WEDNESDAY

BEGIN

Spend a minute or two in silence. Set aside whatever might hinder your prayer.

PRAY

Seek good and not evil so that you may live, and the LORD will be with you.

~Amos 5:14

LISTEN

Read Matthew 9:14–15

Jesus answered them, "Can the wedding guests mourn as long as the bridegroom is with them? The days will come when the bridegroom is taken away from them, and then they will fast."

~Matthew 9:15

Fasting to Feast

Wedding banquets don't usually come to mind when we think about fasting during Lent. I've never seen fish sticks served at a wedding reception, and I've been to more than a few! Nevertheless, when Jesus is challenged about fasting in today's gospel, he responds by calling himself a bridegroom and referring to us, his friends, as his wedding guests. Jesus is saying that being in relationship with him is in many ways like attending a joyful wedding feast.

Jesus wants us to keep this joy in mind as we approach the discipline of fasting. We fast during Lent not primarily to lose weight or to get healthy, not because it's a Catholic cultural badge, and not because we need to prove our holiness to God or anyone else. As Catholics, we give up things for Lent that can become compulsions in our lives in order to grow in freedom, grow a little bit closer to Jesus, and better live the mandates of being his disciples. Anytime we grow a little bit closer to our Lord, the result is joy. Sometimes that joy comes slowly or after a long struggle, but it always comes.

We might say, then, that we fast in order to feast. When we fast, we arrive hungry to the joyful feast of new and abundant life that Jesus pours out upon us.

ACT

I will work at being joyful because I know the Lord is with me. The joy of the children of God is not a shallow pleasantness, but is a life-anchoring surety and undying hope.

PRAY

Lord Jesus, help my fasting to lead me to freedom. Teach me to let go of what distracts me from the joy of being your healing presence in this world. Amen.

Saturday after Ash Wednesday

BEGIN

Spend a minute or two in silence. Set aside whatever might hinder your prayer.

PRAY

I take no pleasure in the death of the wicked man, says the Lord, but rather in his conversion, that he may live.

~Ezekiel 33:11

LISTEN

Read Luke 5:27–32

The Pharisees and their scribes complained to his disciples, saying, "Why do you eat and drink with tax collectors and sinners?" Jesus said to them in reply, "Those who are healthy do not need a physician, but the sick do."

~Luke 5:30–31

A Different Perception

"Two men looked out through prison bars," wrote Oscar Wilde, "One saw mud, the other saw stars." Differences in perception can indeed lead two people to see the same thing, the same event, or the same person in radically dissimilar ways.

Consider today's gospel. Jesus and his critics see Levi very differently. Levi is a tax collector, which many at the time considered a dishonorable profession. That's why the Pharisees see Levi as someone to avoid and condemn. But Jesus perceives him as someone to call to discipleship and to love. The critics demonize Levi as a sinner, while Jesus sees him as one in need of healing.

This dramatic difference of perception leads to a dramatic difference in approach. Levi is shunned by the Pharisees, but summoned by Jesus. They reject, but Jesus recruits. The Pharisees keep Levi at arms' length, while Jesus calls him closer, saying, "Follow me."

Jesus approaches us in exactly the same way. He calls us to follow him, but not because we're perfect. He knows well that we're in need of healing and conversion. He invites us to repentance, but as a response to his love, not so that we might earn it. This gives us both consolation and hope. Jesus does indeed call us to change, but not without first loving us just as we are.

ACT

I will reach out in kindness to someone whom I do not know; who annoys me; or against whom I harbor some dislike or unfair suspicion.

PRAY

Gracious God, teach me this day the power of your love for me and for all people. May I convey your love in all I do and say. Amen.

Sunday, First Week

BEGIN

Spend a minute or two in silence. Set aside whatever might hinder your prayer.

PRAY

One does not live on bread alone, but on every word that comes forth from the mouth of God.

~Matthew 4:4b

LISTEN

Read Luke 4:1–13

Filled with the Holy Spirit, Jesus returned from the Jordan and was led by the Spirit into the desert for forty days, to be tempted by the devil.

~Luke 4:1–2a

Temptations' Silver Lining

Like death and taxes, temptations are an inevitable part of life. Jesus himself was tempted, as today's gospel reminds us. And if he wasn't exempt from temptations, then neither will we be. Yet every cloud has a silver lining. Temptations can be useful because we become more like Jesus when we face them and defeat them.

Temptations invite us to reach out to Jesus and place our trust in him so he can strengthen our resolve and teach us holiness. For instance, we learn patience when we resist the urge to blow our top; we learn love by struggling to love the unlovely; we become humble when we swallow our pride. In other words, temptations are opportunities for growth, not for failure.

We grow through temptations by staying close to the Lord through prayer and sacrament, avoiding near occasions of sin, receiving help from a companion or support group, and seeking to relieve our stress and fatigue—conditions that can make us vulnerable to sin. That's why Jesus' temptations came in a desert, where he was hot, hungry, tired, and alone. The desert is a place of vulnerability, where one could easily fall prey to temptation.

Ironically, one temptation we face is to become impatient with ourselves when we fail to resist temptation. Jesus invites us to be as patient with ourselves as he is with us. His love for us is more powerful than any temptation to sin, if we can but know and accept it. We can forget this and get discouraged, but that's the last thing Jesus wants us to do. As St. Thomas Aquinas assures us: "Christ wished to be tempted, in order to fill us with confidence in his mercy."

ACT

I will identify one sin toward which I am often tempted, like gossip, misplaced or exaggerated anger, holding on to a grudge, or drinking too much. When I find myself being tempted, I will pause and pray, "Lord Jesus Christ, have mercy on me."

PRAY

Lord Jesus, open my heart to your tender mercy, that it may heal me. Give me courage to leave my sin behind and enter more fully into the saving grace of your love. Amen.

Monday, First Week

> *Spend a minute or two in silence. Set aside whatever might hinder your prayer.*

PRAY

> Behold, now is a very acceptable time;
> behold, now is the day of salvation.
>
> ~2 Corinthians 6:2b

LISTEN

> *Read Matthew 25:31–46*

> Then the righteous will answer him and say,
> "Lord, when did we see you ill or in prison, and
> visit you?" And the king will say to them in reply:
> "Amen, I say to you, whatever you did for one of
> these least brothers of mine, you did for me."
>
> ~Matthew 25:37a, 39–40

Invitation to Mercy

A youth minister once shared with me how he'd led a group of young people in song outside a high security prison. After some time, hands were seen sticking wet toilet paper on the prison's small slit windows. Letters emerged, then a complete message: "Pray for us." "We went to visit our brothers in prison," the youth minister explained, "because Jesus was a prisoner too."

As I listened to this, I recalled another conversation, this time with a parish volunteer. Her pastor had asked her to arrange for parish children to stuff Christmas goody bags of toiletries for local inmates. She was appalled and flatly refused, insisting that people being punished for their crimes didn't deserve any goody bags.

What a contrast between these two people, both committed Catholics! They held very different attitudes about the exercise of mercy. In today's gospel, Jesus makes clear what he wants our attitude to be. He speaks of prisoners, the sick, the poor, and strangers—people we might be tempted to judge, condemn, dismiss, or ignore. So often we respond out of unwarranted fear, self-absorption, apathy, or hardness of heart to those who are not like us. Yet Jesus refers to such people as his brothers and explains that we serve him when we serve them. His challenge to us today, then, is to extend mercy to others, just as he has showered his mercy upon us.

ACT

I will try to imagine what life in prison is like. What would it be like to have made very bad choices and ended up there or to be imprisoned because of my beliefs or because of war? I will pray for prisoners, their families, and the victims of crime, political oppression, and war.

PRAY

Gentle God, open my eyes to see the least of my brothers and sisters. May I not fear, judge, or ignore them, but find your face in them and open my heart to their needs. Amen.

Tuesday, First Week

BEGIN

Spend a minute or two in silence. Set aside whatever might hinder your prayer.

PRAY

One does not live on bread alone, but on every word that comes forth from the mouth of God.

~*Matthew 4:4b*

LISTEN

Read Matthew 6:7–15

In praying, do not babble like the pagans, who think that they will be heard because of their many words. Do not be like them. Your Father knows what you need before you ask him.

~*Matthew 6:7–8*

Undivided Attention

A familiar expression, "The squeaky wheel gets the grease," means that annoyingly persistent or pushy people are usually heard and get what they want. Thankfully, as Jesus teaches in today's gospel, we don't need to be a "squeaky wheel" with God. We don't need to pester God to get his attention; we don't need to jump and shout or—to borrow Jesus' phrase—"babble on and on" to get God to hear us. The truth is, God is already listening. He knows what we need even before we ask, because he knows us and loves us better than we know and love ourselves.

Nevertheless, we're invited to ask God for what we need, simply and honestly, for four reasons:

- first, so that we can learn to depend on God, and not on ourselves;

- second, so we can acknowledge that all good things come from God, and give him thanks and praise in return;

- third, so we can share conversation with God about those people and situations that are important to us, which deepens our relationship with him;

- and fourth, because our prayer really and truly changes things.

We might say that God loves to hear our voice! We don't have to raise it or cry out, because we already have his undivided attention. Squeaky wheels are unnecessary. He'll give us all the grease, and the grace, we need.

ACT

I will sit with God in perfect silence for at least five minutes as I might sit with my closest friend when no words are necessary.

PRAY

Lord God, teach me to listen as much as I speak when I pray. Amen.

WEDNESDAY, FIRST WEEK

Spend a minute or two in silence. Set aside whatever might hinder your prayer.

PRAY

Even now, says the LORD, return to me with your whole heart, for I am gracious and merciful.

~*See Joel 2:12–13*

LISTEN

Read Luke 11:29–32

At the judgment the men of Nineveh will arise with this generation and condemn it, because at the preaching of Jonah they repented, and there is something greater than Jonah here.

~*Luke 11:32*

Don't Blame Me!

Most of us are familiar with the term the "Me" generation, which refers loosely to people born in the 1970s through early 1990s. One psychologist, however, refers instead to the "Don't Blame Me" generation. These people, and so many of us, tend to think: "I am more important than most people; I am good; I don't really do bad things." What we have, she concludes, is a generation of people who don't think they need to change anything about themselves. They feel in many ways entitled to do and have what they want, when they want it.

In today's gospel, Jesus speaks about another generation of people who didn't see a need for change. Through his very presence among them, they were presented with something far greater than Solomon's wisdom and Jonah's preaching. Yet still they didn't change; they just didn't see the need. Jesus might very well have directed his words to all of us who tend to hold a "don't blame me" attitude today.

When the Ninevites repented (Jonah 3:1–10), they learned that God, in his compassion and mercy, never spurns a humble and contrite heart. We experience this as well whenever we embrace our need for change and so repent, or turn around and once again face our loving God. So while "don't blame me" may be a common attitude in our culture and the cry of a generation, Jesus invites us to instead make our cry one of faith and humble repentance, "Have mercy on me!"

ACT

I will examine my daily interactions with other people and name one negative habit I would like to break. I will write down two things I can and will do to take responsibility for ending that habit.

PRAY

Lord, humble my heart and my mind. Guide me to true repentance where not only my attitude but also my actions will change to more fully conform to your love. Amen.

Thursday, First Week

Spend a minute or two in silence. Set aside whatever might hinder your prayer.

PRAY

A clean heart create for me, God;
Give me back the joy of your salvation.

~Psalm 51:12a, 14a

LISTEN

Read Matthew 7:7–12

If you then, who are wicked, know how to give good gifts to your children, how much more will your heavenly Father give good things to those who ask him.

~Matthew 7:11

Asking to Receive

"Preaching to the choir" is a familiar expression referring to a message delivered to those who don't really need to hear it. They need no convincing, because they're already convinced. We might think that Jesus is preaching to the choir in today's gospel when he speaks to his chosen disciples about the importance of asking God for the things they need. It seems so obvious! However, we don't always do this, do we?

Sometimes we get so anxious or angry about something that we forget to pray about it. We may fear that asking things from God is kind of selfish, or that our troubles aren't quite worthy of his attention. Maybe deep down we think that God doesn't really deal in details; otherwise, how do we explain bad things happening? Or it could be that sometimes we're just lazy or apathetic or overly self-reliant.

The good news of today's gospel is that God wants to bless us with good things, even though we're far from perfect, because he loves us so much. He knows what we need, and he's ready and happy to give it! It's up to us, however, to ask, not because we can control the divine initiative, but because sharing with God our needs, desires, sorrows, and agonies binds us to him in ways that are essential for those of us who seek to do his will.

ACT

I will think about how I pray—not just in church or at meal times. When and why am I most likely to pray? What good do I really think it does? How can I change my prayer habits or lack thereof?

PRAY

Good and loving God, today I ask . . . Amen.

FRIDAY, FIRST WEEK

BEGIN

Spend a minute or two in silence. Set aside whatever might hinder your prayer.

PRAY

Cast away from you all the crimes you have committed, says the Lord, and make for yourselves a new heart and a new spirit.

~Ezekiel 18:31

LISTEN

Read Matthew 5:20–26

I tell you, unless your righteousness surpasses that of the scribes and Pharisees, you will not enter into the kingdom of heaven.

~Matthew 5:20

A Higher Standard

Have you ever thought: "You know, I'm not a bad person. I haven't robbed a bank or murdered anyone!" For the most part, it's true: we're people of good will who want to do the right thing. We probably haven't been seriously tempted to commit bank robbery or murder.

But good people usually aren't tempted to do really bad things. What they are tempted to do are things that are less good, like settling for a "good enough" morality that's satisfied with not being a bank robber or an ax murderer. For Christians, however, that's just not enough. Our righteousness must exceed that of the scribes and the Pharisees. We're called to a higher standard.

Jesus explains what this involves in today's gospel. He confirms that we aren't to kill anyone, but we also aren't to burn bridges, hurl insults, or feed resentments. Instead, we are to be fence menders—people who reconcile, forgive, and apologize. Has anyone hurt us? We are to forgive them. Have we hurt anyone? Then we need to say we are sorry. Even if that person hurt us back, or hurt us first. And even if we suspect he or she will hurt us again.

We might protest and say: "That's not fair!" And we'd be right if we imagine fairness to mean only that two people or things are treated exactly evenly. But Jesus doesn't call to be fair; he doesn't call us to be "good enough." Jesus calls us to live his Father's justice, which goes far beyond fairness, and he calls us to love others with the same passionate love he has for us.

ACT

I will be more than good enough in my interactions with others today.

PRAY

Almighty God, you have shown us the path to eternal life. Help me to always pursue what is just and reflective of your love.

SATURDAY, FIRST WEEK

BEGIN

Spend a minute or two in silence. Set aside whatever might hinder your prayer.

PRAY

Behold, now is a very acceptable time;
behold, now is the day of salvation.

~2 Corinthians 6:2b

LISTEN

Read Matthew 5:43–48

You have heard that it was said, "You shall love your neighbor and hate your enemy." But I say to you, love your enemies, and pray for those who persecute you, that you may be children of your heavenly Father.

~Matthew 5:43–45a

To See Like Jesus

A retreat leader once put on a pair of cheap sunglasses with white crosses painted on the lenses. His point? To stress that Jesus invites us to see others as he sees them—through the lens of the cross; through the lens of love.

This would include our enemies, as today's gospel makes clear. Jesus knows that when someone threatens us, attacks us, or seriously hurts us, it's easy for us to see that person as nothing more than the source of our pain. We easily demonize him or her, making that person an enemy at best and less than human at worst.

When Jesus invites us to love our enemies, he invites us to see them as he sees them—as God's creation, made in the image of his Heavenly Father. Perhaps the one who hurt us was acting out of pain, ignorance, or illness. He or she is certainly not entirely bad. This is someone for whom Jesus died and who—in spite of whatever they may have done—is nevertheless still desperately loved by God.

This doesn't mean that we can't or shouldn't defend others and ourselves and challenge hurtful behavior. Love often requires that we do so! And love doesn't make us into doormats. But love also leads to other possibilities that hate precludes. Hatred only drives apart. Love can bring together. Only love, and not hate, holds out the potential and the hope for chasms to be bridged, fences to be mended, hurts to be healed, and enemies to become friends.

ACT

I will pray for the one person who has hurt me most in my life and if I have not already done so, I will try to forgive.

PRAY

God of compassion, heal me of any anger or ill will I carry in my heart. I know it may take time and much more prayer, but give me hope and comfort me in your mercy. Amen.

SUNDAY, SECOND WEEK

BEGIN

Spend a minute or two in silence. Set aside whatever might hinder your prayer.

PRAY

From the shining cloud the Father's voice is heard:
This is my beloved Son, hear him.

~*Matthew 17:5*

LISTEN

Read Luke 9:28b–36

About eight days after he said this, Jesus took Peter, John, and James and went up the mountain to pray. While he was praying his face changed in appearance and his clothing became dazzling white.

~*Luke 9:28–29*

Memories of the Mountaintop

Have you ever experienced something that really challenged your faith? Maybe it was the sudden death of a loved one, a serious illness, the loss of a job, a betrayal by a spouse, the horror of war, or the heartbreaking realities of poverty. Maybe a combination of things led you to question God's love, or even God's very existence.

In today's gospel story, three of the closest followers of Jesus witness his transfiguration. Perhaps Jesus knew that his death would challenge their faith and so he wanted to keep them close and give them something to hold on to during and after his crucifixion. Surely what they experienced on that mountain gave them hope that Jesus' death wasn't the final word, and helped them trust that there was something better yet to come.

When facing a crisis of faith, we can find hope by recalling those times when God has touched our lives and revealed some of his goodness and power to us. We might remember a prayer answered, an uplifting brush with grace, a time scripture spoke directly to our hearts, or an instance when God used a situation or another person to guide our lives in a certain direction. And we can always bring to mind what Jesus did for us during his ministry on earth. When we recall and reflect on these things, our faith and courage are shored up.

Should our faith get shaken, Jesus wants us to remember that he loves us, is always with us, has a plan for us, brings good out of evil, and that his greatest wish is that we spend all eternity with him.

ACT

I will keep in mind the memory of a time when I felt certain that God was with me. In my gratitude, I will let hope rule my heart when I am tempted to be discouraged, frustrated, or apathetic.

PRAY

Lord Jesus, help me to understand the power of prayer in times of crisis and in times of great joy. Most of all, teach me to pray every day, even when my need is not great nor my joy overwhelming. Amen.

MONDAY, SECOND WEEK

BEGIN

Spend a minute or two in silence. Set aside whatever might hinder your prayer.

PRAY

Your words, Lord, are Spirit and life;
you have the words of everlasting life.

~John 6:63c, 68c

LISTEN

Read Luke 6:36–38

Jesus said to his disciples: "Be merciful, just as your Father is merciful. Stop judging and you will not be judged. Stop condemning and you will not be condemned."

~Luke 6:36

A Dangerous Double Standard

When a car speeds past us on the highway, we easily label the driver a "jerk," or something worse. But when we're the one who's speeding, it's because we're in a hurry for a very important reason. We condemn others but excuse ourselves for doing exactly the same thing. We reason that we act with the best of motives, but assume that others do not. Why? Because we evaluate ourselves based on our *intentions*, but judge others based on their *behavior*.

Jesus cautions us in today's gospel about applying this double standard; he warns us against judging others. Yes, we can judge if another person's *actions* are right or wrong, or if his or her thoughts are true or false, as we have measuring rods for doing that. But we can't judge the person because we can't see into his or her heart. Only God can do that, and he is far wiser, and more merciful, than we ever could be.

Instead of judging, Jesus calls us to imitate the compassion, forgiveness, and generosity of God the Father. He invites us, in the words of Blessed Charles de Foucauld: "Do unto others, as you would have *God* do unto you." This goes a step beyond the Golden Rule, which urges us to treat others as we want them to treat us. Making the activity of God the standard of our own behavior leads us to a life worthy of the name Christian.

ACT

When others annoy me today, I will pause to consider what they might be facing. I will not judge, but instead show kindness.

PRAY

Lord God, pour out your mercy upon me and let it change my heart. Renew within me a spirit of compassion, that I may always deal kindly with others and show them your love. Amen.

TUESDAY, SECOND WEEK

BEGIN

Spend a minute or two in silence. Set aside whatever might hinder your prayer.

PRAY

Cast away from you all the crimes you have committed, says the Lord, and make for yourselves a new heart and a new spirit.

~Ezekiel 18:31

LISTEN

Read Matthew 23:1–12

Therefore, do and observe all things whatsoever they tell you, but do not follow their example. Whoever exalts himself will be humbled; but whoever humbles himself will be exalted.

~Matthew 23:3, 12

Standing Together before Jesus

When my young son asked about a certain word he'd heard, I explained that he shouldn't use it under any circumstances. "But Dad," he objected, "I've heard you use it!" Oops . . . I'd taught him: "Do as I say, but not as I do."

I was like the religious leaders in today's gospel who didn't practice what they preached. But that might be said about any of us. Most of us have been guilty of talking the talk without walking the walk. Sometimes we realize this and don't "preach" at all, when actually we should be saying something. For instance, parents might avoid speaking about sex or drinking or drugs with their children, because their own histories are less than perfect. They've made mistakes and perhaps have regrets, which cause them to shy away from talking with their children about what is right and wrong.

So what are we to do? If we say something, others might roll their eyes; but if we say nothing, they might turn their eyes elsewhere and discover the wrong answers. Thankfully, Jesus suggests a way forward when he speaks of humility in today's gospel. We can admit that we're less than perfect, and place ourselves beside those we instruct, instead of exalting ourselves above them. We all stand before Christ as students before our teacher, servants before our master, sinners before our savior. If we do this, what others will most likely hear is: "Do as *Jesus* says we all should do—not as *I* sometimes do."

ACT

I will make a difference in my world today by speaking up for what is right. This may be a personal matter with a family member or friend. Or it might be getting involved in a social issue where I can stand up for justice. I will remember that I don't have to be perfect in order to remind others to do the right thing.

PRAY

All-knowing God, humble my heart enough to know that in challenging others to do what is right, I also challenge myself. Amen.

WEDNESDAY, SECOND WEEK

BEGIN

Spend a minute or two in silence. Set aside whatever might hinder your prayer.

PRAY

I am the light of the world, says the Lord;
whoever follows me will have the light of life.

~John 8:12

LISTEN

Read Matthew 20:17–28

But Jesus summoned them and said, "You know that the rulers of the Gentiles lord it over them, and the great ones make their authority over them felt. But it shall not be so among you. Rather, whoever wishes to be great among you shall be your servant; whoever wishes to be first among you shall be your slave."

~Matthew 20:25–27

Nice Guys Don't Finish Last

In our dog-eat-dog world, it doesn't seem to matter who gets trampled upon or left behind in the struggle for power and influence. Such selfish behavior is excused by statements like, "It's not personal, it's business," or "Nice guys finish last."

But are those statements really true? Not according to Jesus in today's gospel. He had just told his disciples about his impending torture and execution when the sons of Zebedee, along with their mother, make a power grab. They likely thought: "Jesus' time is short, so we'd better make our move to be on top in his kingdom. *Carpe diem*; you snooze, you lose." They don't express any real comprehension or concern about Jesus' fate or seem to care what their friends might think. Their selfish ambition seems to have blinded them to compassion or concern for anyone else.

Jesus turns this situation into a teachable moment. He concedes that the world may seem to belong to those who can swim with the sharks. But as his disciples, we are to swim against the tide. He invites us to follow in his footsteps by living a life of service; by being focused on others' needs; by being humble; and by cherishing sacrifice, not selfishness.

The world may indeed delude us into thinking that "nice guys finish last." Except, Jesus reminds us, in the race that really counts.

ACT

I will be mindful of my ambitions and ask myself toward what end they lead me. If the end is not in line with Gospel values, I will begin to redirect those ambitions.

PRAY

Gentle Lord, teach me humility and clarity of purpose. Help me remember that it is often not as important to meet my goals, even those befitting a Christian, as it is to work toward those goals with true Christian charity. Amen.

Thursday, Second Week

BEGIN

Spend a minute or two in silence. Set aside whatever might hinder your prayer.

PRAY

Blessed are they who have kept the word with a generous heart and yield a harvest through perseverance.

~Luke 8:15

LISTEN

Read Luke 16:19–31

And lying at his door was a poor man named Lazarus, covered with sores, who would gladly have eaten his fill of the scraps that fell from the rich man's table.

~Luke 16:20

Opportunities to Love

If you found on your doorstep a filthy, starving, homeless man surrounded by stray dogs, how would you react? Would you see an opportunity to love, heal, and serve? Would you see the face of Christ in the man? Or would you be repulsed, scared, or annoyed? Would you try to ignore him and hope that he'd go away?

That's what the rich man in today's gospel did. It's not that he couldn't see Lazarus; he was simply too hard of heart to help. He separated himself from the plight of Lazarus his neighbor—a separation that continued after they died, except with a dramatic reversal of fortune.

Jesus told this parable to challenge our way of thinking about the poor, so that we can change our way of acting. Jesus invites us to see the Lazaruses on our doorstep as brothers and sisters, not burdens; as opportunities, not inconveniences; as persons, not problems.

He's not asking us to do the impossible, but to do what we can. Lazarus would have welcomed table scraps—a reminder that even the small things we do can seem so great to those who have so little. As St. Anselm once said: "The fasts of the rich are the feasts of the poor."

ACT

I will look again at the commitment to almsgiving I wrote down on Ash Wednesday. Have I kept that resolution? If not, how can I get back on track with it, or amend it to ensure that I will do something this Lent for those in need?

PRAY

Merciful Christ, open my eyes to the poor in my community and in the world. Do not let me turn away from or simply avoid their need. Give me the courage and determination to help them and to speak up for the protection of their human dignity. Amen.

FRIDAY, SECOND WEEK

BEGIN

Spend a minute or two in silence. Set aside whatever might hinder your prayer.

PRAY

God so loved the world that he gave his only-begotten Son; so that everyone who believes in him might have eternal life.

~John 3:16

LISTEN

Read Matthew 21:33–43, 45–46

Finally, he sent his son to them, thinking, "They will respect my son." But when the tenants saw the son, they said to one another, "This is the heir. Come, let us kill him and acquire his inheritance."

~Matthew 21:37–38

Deeply and Madly

People in love sometimes do crazy things, and that's true for God, too. Not that God is *crazy*, but he is crazy *in love* with us. Think about today's gospel, in which a landowner's servants are attacked when they go to collect the rent. If we were the landowner, we'd most likely call the police and our lawyers. But this landowner sends even more servants and they too are attacked. Finally, the landowner sends his own son, hoping that he of all people will be respected.

The landowner, of course, is analogous to God the Father, his servants to the prophets, and his son to Jesus. The tenants are analogous to the leaders of the Chosen People. At one level, then, this story is about the rejection of Jesus. But at another level, how the landowner treats those tenants says to us that God is crazy about us, the people he loves. It says that God is patient with us; that God sees the potential for growth in us; and that God gives us not just second and third chances, but innumerable chances. With God, strict justice takes a backseat to abundant compassion and mercy.

Yes, we hear about the tenants being put to death. Yet those aren't Jesus' words, but somebody else's. The only death Jesus speaks of is his own—a death for their sakes and ours, a death that could only be embraced by one who is crazy in love.

ACT

I will identify one failing in my life that I seem to keep repeating and come up with a new plan to overcome it. When I am tempted to this sin, I will instead thank God for the chance to turn away from it, and then do so.

PRAY

God of mercy and compassion, sustain me in this season of repentance. Help me respond to you as one who knows and loves me as no one else can, not as one who is distant and out of touch. Amen.

Saturday, Second Week

Spend a minute or two in silence. Set aside whatever might hinder your prayer.

PRAY

I will get up and go to my father and shall say to him, "Father, I have sinned against heaven and against you."

~Luke 15:18

LISTEN

Read Luke 15:1–3, 11–32

He said to him, "My son, you are here with me always; everything I have is yours. But now we must celebrate and rejoice, because your brother was dead and has come to life again; he was lost and has been found."

~Luke 15:31–32

Becoming the Father

With which character in the Parable of the Prodigal Son do you most identify? Is it the elder brother, angry that his wayward sibling was welcomed home with a party? He feels entitled to more, ripped off, unappreciated, and jealous. He is dutiful but dour; reliable but resentful.

Perhaps you resonate with the younger brother, who blew his money, hurt the ones he should have loved, and did cocky, foolish, and sinful things that later filled him with shame and regret. He had to hit rock bottom before he began to get his act together.

Or maybe it's the father you feel closest to: concerned about his children, sharing wisdom with patience, celebrating the joys of life, and welcoming those he loves, regardless of how badly they may have treated him.

It's likely the two brothers describe who all of us are, or who we have been, and that the father is a model of who we wish we were, who we'd like to be. Yes, the father does represent God the Father. But he also represents who the Father calls us to become: one who shares love and forgiveness with others in the way he shares them with us.

The Father invites us to imagine ourselves, not with arms crossed in anger or with head downcast and shoulders slumped, but with arms open wide, ready to welcome those who have wronged us and to offer forgiveness.

ACT

> I will reflect on how much I am like or unlike the father in this gospel story. If I am very different from him, how can I change?

PRAY

> Father of forgiveness, instill in me a deep desire to be like you. Teach me to respond to others with compassion, always ready to forgive and to love. Amen.

SUNDAY, THIRD WEEK

BEGIN

Spend a minute or two in silence. Set aside whatever might hinder your prayer.

PRAY

Repent, says the Lord; the kingdom of heaven is at hand.

~Matthew 4:17

LISTEN

Read Luke 13:1–9

And he told them this parable: "There once was a person who had a fig tree planted in his orchard, and when he came in search of fruit on it but found none, he said to the gardener, 'For three years now I have come in search of fruit on this fig tree but have found none. So cut it down. Why should it exhaust the soil?'"

~Luke 13:6–7

Receiving and Giving

Whenever Election Day approaches, politicians ask us the question: "Are you better off than you were four years ago?" As Christians we must also ask, "Are the poor better off than they were four years ago?" Whether we're discussing politics or something else, our Lord calls us to be concerned with more than just our own welfare. He tells us to look beyond our needs and consider the needs of others; to understand and protect the common good and not just whatever we think will be good for us; to be givers, not just takers; to be other-directed, not self-centered.

This seems to be Jesus' message in today's gospel. He tells the parable of a tree that bore no fruit, even though it had been given plenty of time and careful attention. In frustration, the landowner asks the gardener, "Why should it exhaust the soil any longer?" In other words, why should it continue to receive, when it doesn't want to give? This is a question we can pose to ourselves in light of all that God has given to us.

The landowner's question is certainly a challenge, because it's deeply counter-cultural. Just think about it: the world encourages greed, Jesus calls for generosity; the world speaks of self-gratification, Jesus speaks of self-giving; the world seeks self-fulfillment, Jesus asks for self-sacrifice. The world rejects those who don't measure up to the status quo, but Jesus calls for compassion.

God has given us all so much, and all his gifts are absolutely free. We are to be generous stewards of all we've been given, and God will hold us accountable to that calling. As St. Catherine of Siena once wrote, "From what you have received, give!"

ACT

What habit or behavior in my life seems to be taking up my time, energy, or other resources, but bearing little fruit? I will attend to this today, asking whether I should let it go or give it one more try to produce good fruit.

PRAY

Heavenly Father, you who forgive my sin, teach me to tend the garden of my soul. Help me prune away all that does not bring forth the good fruit of your love and mercy and learn to nurture all that does. Amen.

Monday, Third Week

BEGIN

Spend a minute or two in silence. Set aside whatever might hinder your prayer.

PRAY

I hope in the LORD, I trust in his word;
with him there is kindness and plenteous
redemption.

~Psalm 130:5, 7

LISTEN

Read Luke 4:24–30

Jesus said to the people in the synagogue at Nazareth: "Amen, I say to you, no prophet is accepted in his own native place."

~Luke 4:24

Can You Hear Me Now?

One cell phone ad campaign features a character in all sorts of remote places asking into his phone, "Can you hear me now?" The implication is that if he were using another cell phone provider, his words would have fallen on deaf ears. It's frustrating when others fail to hear what we have to say, for whatever reason.

In today's gospel reading, Jesus gives two examples of God's people refusing to hear God's word as spoken by the prophets Elijah and Elisha. People didn't like God's word when Jesus spoke it either, and they tried to kill him for it.

All of us are guilty of failing to listen to God's word. Maybe our Lord is challenging us through today's gospel to ask ourselves what it is we don't want to hear, won't allow ourselves to hear, or are failing to hear because we just aren't listening at all. Is it about money? Forgiveness? Our use of time? Sex? Are we too proud to hear? Too angry? Too indifferent? Too addicted?

Perhaps we can all use the remainder of Lent to truly open our ears to God, so that should he say to us, "Can you hear me now?" our answer will be an emphatic "Yes, Lord, I can!"

ACT

I will take an honest look at my life today and ask myself in what area God may be trying to reach me, but about which I don't want to hear. I will pray to be open to the Lord.

PRAY

Merciful Lord, cleanse my heart of stubborn unwillingness to hear your word and repent. Let me listen and be saved. Amen.

TUESDAY, THIRD WEEK

BEGIN

Spend a minute or two in silence. Set aside whatever might hinder your prayer.

PRAY

Even now, says the Lord, return to me with your whole heart; for I am gracious and merciful.

~Joel 2:12–13

LISTEN

Read Matthew 18:21–35

Peter approached Jesus and asked him, "Lord, if my brother sins against me, how often must I forgive him? As many as seven times?" Jesus answered, "I say to you, not seven times but seventy-seven times."

~Matthew 18:21–22

More than Three Strikes

St. Peter never played baseball. Nevertheless, "Three strikes and you're out!" seemed to be the operative model when he asked Jesus about forgiveness. As we're often tempted to do, Peter assumed that there's a limit to the forgiveness we can reasonably be expected to give, be it once, three times, or seven times. Jesus understood this. That's why he stressed that those who follow him are to forgive "seventy-seven times." In other words, we are to forgive without limit.

Jesus doesn't say that we need to condone what was done to us, deny our pain, or trust the person who harmed us. However, he does call us to make the decision to forgive, and free ourselves from resentment and the desire for revenge.

When we refuse to forgive, we contribute to the world's sorrow, and there's enough of that already. We demonize the person who wronged us, and that's unfair to them. And we deny ourselves the gift of God's forgiveness, which is foolishness to us.

Forgiveness is often really hard and can take a long time to do completely. But Jesus shows us the way and helps us along the way. After all, he doesn't call us to give to others anything he's not first given to us.

ACT

I will examine my life and determine to forgive anyone who has caused the nagging hurts I feel. I will keep in mind that sometimes I think I've forgiven and moved on, only to discover that I need to forgive the same person again and again, for the same hurt, because Jesus says, "seventy-seven times."

PRAY

Lord Jesus Christ, help me to forgive both the things that hurt me most and the little annoyances of every day. Amen.

WEDNESDAY, THIRD WEEK

BEGIN

Spend a minute or two in silence. Set aside whatever might hinder your prayer.

PRAY

Your words, Lord, are Spirit and life;
you have the words of everlasting life.

~John 6:63c, 68c

LISTEN

Read Matthew 5:17–19

Therefore, whoever breaks one of the least of these commandments and teaches others to do so will be called least in the kingdom of heaven. But whoever obeys and teaches these commandments will be called greatest in the kingdom of heaven.

~Matthew 5:19

Read the Fine Print

"Always read the fine print" is good advice that we don't always follow. We typically put "always read the fine print" in the same category as "rinse and repeat" and "do not insert cotton swab into the ear canal!" In today's gospel, however, Jesus tells us that we do indeed need to read the fine print when it comes to God's law.

Jesus promises us that until the end of time, not an iota, not a dot of God's law will pass away. He explains that he will not abolish even the smallest part of it, as some of his contemporaries fear or perhaps hope.

But we might ask ourselves: Who would want this law to pass away? Who would wish to see it abolished?

God's law is his gift to us. To keep it is to keep close to God, and it is the only sure path to human happiness, wholeness, and fulfillment. And let's be honest: Who among us doesn't want to be happy, whole, and fulfilled? Who doesn't want God to be close? Deep down, this is what we all want, because God has made us this way. That's why Jesus said that those who keep and teach God's law are truly great in the kingdom of God. Indeed, when it comes to God's law, we should always read the fine print.

ACT

When Jesus refers to "the law" and "the prophets," he means the whole of God's revelation in the Old Testament. I will use my bible to learn something new about the Old Testament.

PRAY

Loving God, Creator of heaven and earth, keep me ever faithful to your commands so that I may know and love you more fully and serve your kingdom here on earth. Amen.

Thursday, Third Week

BEGIN

Spend a minute or two in silence. Set aside whatever might hinder your prayer.

PRAY

Even now, says the Lord, return to me with your whole heart, for I am gracious and merciful.

~*Joel 2:12–13*

LISTEN

Read Luke 11:14–23

Whoever is not with me is against me, and whoever does not gather with me scatters.

~*Luke 11:23*

Choosing Sides

Are you with me or against me? This is the choice Jesus presents to us in today's gospel. Jesus performs a miraculous healing. Critics say his action is evil and Jesus counters that it is a sign of the kingdom of God. Then he says we need to choose whose side we're on. If you think about it, this is a choice we need to make every day, and often several times a day.

On our worst days, we reject Jesus altogether. We tune him out or turn our backs. On other days, however, we do want to stand with Jesus . . . but only on our terms. In other words:

- We're willing to sacrifice—within reasonable limits.

- We're willing to forgive—those people who are truly sorry.

- We're willing to love—those people we like.

- We're willing to give—so long as we receive.

- We're happy to follow Jesus—as long as he goes where we want him to go.

Today's gospel reminds us that we can't have it both ways. As Jesus said, the kingdom of God has indeed come upon us. And we need to choose to follow our king, without limit and without compromise.

ACT

I will choose one of the Christian virtues mentioned above and be especially mindful of living it well today.

PRAY

Jesus, Lord and Savior, help me to stand with you in my words and in my actions as together we do the work of your kingdom. Amen.

FRIDAY, THIRD WEEK

BEGIN

Spend a minute or two in silence. Set aside whatever might hinder your prayer.

PRAY

Repent, says the Lord; the kingdom of heaven is at hand.

~Matthew 4:17

LISTEN

Read Mark 12:28–34

"Which is the first of all the commandments?" Jesus replied, "The first is this: Hear, O Israel! The Lord our God is Lord alone! You shall love the Lord your God with all your heart, with all your soul, with all your mind, and with all your strength. The second is this: You shall love your neighbor as yourself. There is no other commandment greater than these."

~Mark 12:28b–31

Difficult to Love

Who is it today that you're finding difficult to love? Is it someone at home, on the job, in the neighborhood, at church, in the public spotlight? Whoever it may be, today's gospel challenges us to go the extra mile to love that person.

As we read, a scribe asked Jesus what he thought was the *first* of all the commandments. But Jesus didn't just give him the first, which is the commandment to love God above all else. Jesus also gave him the *second*, which is the commandment to love our neighbor as ourselves. Jesus did this because we cannot love God if we don't love our neighbor, nor can we love our neighbor without the love of God.

But just how are we to love? What are we supposed to do? St. Thomas Aquinas said, "Love is wanting what is best for a person and doing what you reasonably can to bring goodness and good things to that person."

Applying this to the person we're finding it difficult to love will take different forms, depending on the circumstances. We may need to exercise patience, swallow our pride, offer forgiveness, be intentionally kind, give them some type of help, or make amends for something hurtful we may have done to them. But regardless of what we might need to do to love difficult people, love them we must if we wish to be people who truly love God.

ACT

I will do two loving things today for someone I find hard to love.

PRAY

O God, in your goodness, strengthen my will to love and deepen my understanding of how to do so. May I learn to love with the whole of my being. Amen.

Saturday, Third Week

Spend a minute or two in silence. Set aside whatever might hinder your prayer.

PRAY

If today you hear his voice, harden not your hearts.

~Psalm 95:8

LISTEN

Read Luke 18:9–14

But the tax collector stood off at a distance and would not even raise his eyes to heaven but beat his breast and prayed, "O God, be merciful to me a sinner." I tell you, the latter went home justified, not the former; for everyone who exalts himself will be humbled, and the one who humbles himself will be exalted.

~Luke 18:13–14

A Humble Proposal

When the tax collector in today's gospel reading cries, "O God, be merciful to me, a sinner!" he isn't beating up on himself. He is being humble. And that's why Jesus invites us to follow his example. Humility doesn't mean that we put ourselves down or cling to low opinions of ourselves. It means that we know the real us—who we are in the eyes of God. In other words, humility is healthy self-knowledge. Pride, on the other hand, is self-deception.

Humility brings us face to face with our shortcomings and failings, and thus our need for God. It enables us to see others with empathy and compassion. Pride too often makes us look down on others in contempt, like the Pharisee in this story. It can even lead us to completely lose sight of our need for God.

By calling us to humility, Jesus invites us to acknowledge our need for change, which is a message of hope, not judgment. The Christian life calls us to stand before God, utterly aware of who we are as his beloved children. Like the tax collector, we are indeed sinners. But we're not sinners in the hands of an angry God. We are sinners in the arms of a merciful God who calls us to embrace humility, that we might be embraced by his love.

ACT

I will try to imagine how I look in the eyes of God.
I will be grateful for the good things I see and
pray for guidance in the areas of my life that need
correcting.

PRAY

Merciful God, I pray for the gift of true humility.
May I seek and find it in my work, in my relation-
ships, and in my prayer. Purify my heart, Lord, that
I may learn empathy and compassion toward all
those I meet. Amen.

Sunday, Fourth Week

BEGIN

Spend a minute or two in silence. Set aside whatever might hinder your prayer.

PRAY

I will get up and go to my Father and shall say to him: Father, I have sinned against heaven and against you.

~Luke 15:18

LISTEN

Read Luke 15:1–3, 11–32

The servant said to him, "Your brother has returned and your father has slaughtered the fattened calf because he has him back safe and sound." He became angry, and when he refused to enter the house, his father came out and pleaded with him. He said to him, "My son, you are here with me always; everything I have is yours. But now we must celebrate and rejoice, because your brother was dead and has come to life again; he was lost and has been found."

~Luke 15:27–28, 31–32

Forgiving Our Families

It's easy to understand the elder brother in the Parable of the Prodigal Son. He feels insulted when his wayward brother is welcomed home with an extravagant party. Never has he publicly shamed his father, blown his inheritance, or indulged in disgraceful behavior. He has always been dependable, but has never been given even a goat for a gathering with his friends.

His feelings can resonate with us whenever we wrestle with family resentments, which can run very deep. We might recall a time when we've been hurt or ignored. Children often grow resentful about how their parents raised them, and parents grow disappointed in children who fail to meet their expectations. Bitter sibling rivalry is not uncommon. Anything related to money, like wills and inheritance, can lead to resentment, as can religion or politics. And then there are issues with in-laws—no need to elaborate there!

Whenever we feel like the elder brother, Jesus invites us to imitate the father instead, who received his son home with forgiveness, not resentment. The elder brother in us may protest that forgiveness isn't fair! But then, Christianity isn't about strict "fairness" as the world understands it. It *is* about justice, but a Christian justice tempered by mercy and grace. Simply understood, justice means "getting what you deserve." Mercy means "not getting what you deserve." And grace means "getting what you don't deserve." Forgiveness isn't deserved either. It is a gift, and it heals. May it bless our families.

ACT

> I will call to mind and pray in gratitude for at least one time when I have known forgiveness. I will ask God's blessing on those who forgave me.

PRAY

> All-loving God, accept my prayer of thanks and praise. Open my heart to your tender mercy and grant me healing forgiveness for all of my sins. Amen.

MONDAY, FOURTH WEEK

BEGIN

Spend a minute or two in silence. Set aside whatever might hinder your prayer.

PRAY

Seek good and not evil so that you may live,
and the Lord will be with you.

~Amos 5:14

LISTEN

Read John 4:43–54

He asked them when he began to recover. They
told him, "The fever left him yesterday, about one
in the afternoon." The father realized that just at
that time Jesus had said to him, "Your son will
live," and he and his whole household came to
believe.

~John 4:52–53

Meeting Us Wherever We Are

Sir Alec Guinness, the famous actor, made what he
called a "negative bargain" with God when his son
contracted polio. If his son recovered, Guinness prom-
ised, he wouldn't hinder his son's wish to become
Catholic. The boy recovered, and Guinness kept his
promise. A few years later, Guinness himself became
Catholic.

Some might take a cynical view of Guinness's
attempt to lure God to the bargaining table. After all,
he turned to God only when he had nowhere else to
turn. Yet that's been the experience of so many of us.
Often it's only when our backs are pressed against the

wall that we give God any real consideration. But God can work with that. He knows that it's when we've hit rock bottom that we're most receptive to his grace.

We see this in today's gospel. The royal official approaches Jesus in desperation, with no other motive than to secure the healing of his dying son. Jesus knows this. "Unless you people see signs and wonders," he observes, "you do not believe." The royal official doesn't contest the point. He simply continues to beg Jesus. And Jesus heals his son, whereupon the official's entire household become believers.

God will meet us wherever we are, because even more than we might desire to be with God, God desires to be with us.

ACT

I will identify the most difficult challenge or deepest wound I face right now and spend five minutes in wordless prayer, letting God be with me in the struggle.

PRAY

God of steadfast love, teach me to cling to you not only through my hardships but in my deepest joys as well. Be my light and strength this day. Amen.

TUESDAY, FOURTH WEEK

BEGIN

Spend a minute or two in silence. Set aside whatever might hinder your prayer.

PRAY

A clean heart create for me, O God;
give me back the joy of your salvation.

~Psalm 51:12a, 14a

LISTEN

Read John 5:1–16

They asked him, "Who is the man who told you, 'Take it up and walk?'" The man who was healed did not know who it was, for Jesus had slipped away, since there was a crowd there.

~John 5:12–13

Just Because We Can

"Practice random acts of kindness" is a popular slogan that challenges us to engage others all around us in ways other than those that serve our own desire to get ahead or be noticed. When we're always working at success or recognition, stopping to perform a small kindness can knock us off schedule; reputations and bottom lines aren't necessarily enhanced by random, unrecognized deeds of kindness.

Consider, however, what Jesus does in today's gospel. He sees a pool full of sick and disabled people. In the world's eyes, they have nothing much to offer and have likely been avoided by most as public embarrassments. Nevertheless, Jesus stops and speaks with a man who has been by the pool for thirty-eight years.

The man says he wants to be healed but cannot reach the water. So Jesus heals him, and then vanishes into the crowd before others take much notice.

Why does Jesus do this? First of all, he does this because he has the power to do so. Likewise, every one of us, with our time, talent, and treasure, is able to do much to bring healing to our world—perhaps more than we often realize or want to admit.

Second, Jesus heals the man because Jesus is humble. It would have been easy for him to draw attention to himself by his miracle. Yet Jesus acts discreetly and without fanfare.

Third, Jesus acts purely out of love, because there is nothing to gain in return for healing this man. Jesus doesn't even receive a "thank you" for his efforts; the man he healed doesn't even know Jesus' name.

Our Lord invites us today to follow his example by doing random acts of kindness with humility and out of love, just because we can.

ACT

Before I finish this devotion, I will identify one person whose life I can make better today by a small act of kindness. Before this time tomorrow, I will do this.

PRAY

Gentle Lord, make bloom in me the joy of kindness and teach me to practice it with humility and love. Amen.

WEDNESDAY, FOURTH WEEK

BEGIN

Spend a minute or two in silence. Set aside whatever might hinder your prayer.

PRAY

I am the resurrection and the life, says the Lord; whoever believes in me will never die.

~John 11:25a, 26

LISTEN

Read John 5:17–30

Jesus answered the Jews:
"My Father is at work until now, so I am at work."
For this reason they tried all the more to kill him, because he not only broke the Sabbath but he also called God his own father, making himself equal to God.

~John 5:17–18

Holding Us Close

Many people are quite comfortable calling their fathers-in-law "Dad." Others, however, find that to be awkward or inappropriate. The very prospect makes them uneasy. Sometimes we can feel uncomfortable about calling God our "Father," or certainly "Dad," as Jesus did. In fact, this so outrages our Lord's critics in today's gospel that they want to kill him! Calling God "Father" hopefully doesn't infuriate us like that, but it sure can make many of us feel uncomfortable.

We can be fine praying to "Almighty God," as that title reflects God's distance from us. But "Father" speaks of God's nearness; for most of us it implies love, family, and an intimate connection. And that might scare us because we worry about getting too close to God. After all, who knows what *that* might lead to? We wonder: "What will God ask of me? What demands could he make? How might my life have to change?" It can seem easier, and a whole lot safer, to keep God at arm's length—almighty on his heavenly throne, way "up there" somewhere.

Jesus challenges us to move beyond our fears. As our brother, he wants us to know the Father not only as one who dwells in heaven, but also as one who abides within us. The same life and love the Father gives to Jesus is also offered to us. Our Father doesn't want to be kept at arm's length. Instead, he wants to hold us in his loving arms.

ACT

I will talk with my earthly father, or someone who is a positive father figure to me. I will take a few minutes before the day is over to reflect on how this person reveals God the Father's love to me.

PRAY

Heavenly Father, gather me in your loving embrace and be my guardian from all harm. Amen.

Thursday, Fourth Week

BEGIN

Spend a minute or two in silence. Set aside whatever might hinder your prayer.

PRAY

God so loved the world that he gave his only-begotten Son, so that everyone who believes in him might have eternal life.

~John 3:16

LISTEN

Read John 5:31–47

The works that the Father gave me to accomplish, these works that I perform testify on my behalf that the Father has sent me. Moreover, the Father who sent me has testified on my behalf. But you have never heard his voice nor seen his form, and you do not have his word remaining in you, because you do not believe in the one whom he has sent.

~John 5:36b–38

From Doubt to Trust

One evening, my wife Stephanie prayed about whether she should return to work. The next morning, a perfect job practically fell into her lap. To us, this was an obvious sign from God. Yet that night, as we adjusted our budget to reflect Stephanie's new income, we started to worry about money, as finances until then had been a bit tight. God had just answered our prayer and shown his care for us. But still we didn't get it; still we didn't trust.

Sadly, that's all too common, as reflected in today's gospel in which we encounter those who refuse to believe in Jesus, even though they are surrounded by evidence that he is the one sent by the Father. In spite of everything, they just don't "get it." God has done so many good things for them, but still they doubt, reject, or simply forget about him.

Sometimes we're guilty of the same things. When times are hard, we begin to doubt God's love and care for us. And when times are good, we easily forget about God altogether, and replace him with the idols of success, beauty, security, and wealth. We do this even after God has done so many good things for us, things that should make us "get it," and call forth our obedience, our trust, and most of all, our love.

ACT

I will examine my life for the one concern that I find most difficult to trust God with. How can I let go and place my faith in God's abiding love for me?

PRAY

Gracious God, help me let go of trying to control life and instead learn to accept its surprising twists and turns. Help me see you in the unexpected events of my life and contemplate you in its deep mysteries. Amen.

FRIDAY, FOURTH WEEK

BEGIN

Spend a minute or two in silence. Set aside whatever might hinder your prayer.

PRAY

One does not live on bread alone, but on every word that comes forth from the mouth of God.

~Matthew 4:4b

LISTEN

Read John 7:1–2, 10, 25–30

Some of the inhabitants of Jerusalem said, "Is he not the one they are trying to kill?
And look, he is speaking openly and they say nothing to him. Could the authorities have realized that he is the Christ? But we know where he is from. When the Christ comes, no one will know where he is from."

~John 7:25–27

Elephants in Mouse Swimsuits

It's easier for an elephant to fit into a mouse's swimsuit, I once heard it explained, than it is for God to fit into our ideas about him. This is an intentionally silly observation, but it's certainly true, especially in light of today's gospel.

The people of Jerusalem think that they have Jesus all figured out. They are convinced that he isn't the Christ, because they know where he came from. But Jesus stops teaching and cries out to them to set them straight.

Jesus sometimes has to do the same thing with us. We create idols—caricatures of Jesus—and he has to come along to displace them. Usually, like the mouse's swimsuit, our image of Jesus is just too small. We tend to emphasize one aspect of his person and minimize the others. For instance, we might count upon his mercy, but forget about his justice. We focus on Jesus' power, but overlook his humility. We highlight his humanity, but neglect his divinity, or vice versa.

However, whenever we think we have him locked up in a nutshell description, the real Jesus eludes us, just as he slipped away from the angry Jerusalem mob. He knows that we're always tempted to refashion him in our own image. Thankfully, he never stops trying to re-create *us* in his.

ACT

I will list on paper all the words I can think of to describe Jesus. Then I'll circle my favorites and contemplate why I am most drawn to those particular words.

PRAY

Lord Jesus, grant me the humility to know that I can never fully comprehend you. Even still, help me to seek you as you truly are rather than who I want you to be. Amen.

Saturday, Fourth Week

BEGIN

BEGIN

> *Spend a minute or two in silence. Set aside whatever might hinder your prayer.*

PRAY

> Blessed are they who have kept the word with a generous heart and yield a harvest through perseverance.
>
> *~Luke 8:15*

LISTEN

> *Read John 7:40–53*
>
> The guards answered, "Never before has anyone spoken like this man." So the Pharisees answered them, "Have you also been deceived? Have any of the authorities or the Pharisees believed in him?"
>
> *~John 7:46–48*

Distracting Voices

Whether they are seductive whispers or violent shouts, distracting voices can keep us from hearing the things we really want or need to hear—including the voice of God. Just consider today's gospel. "Never before has anyone spoken like this man!" the guards exclaim after hearing Jesus. But the Pharisees mock them for believing something they themselves could not.

Are there voices that keep us from hearing God's word, or accepting it for what it is? Maybe it's the alluring voices of our marketing culture, encouraging us to find happiness in the things we buy or in how we look: "Look at me! Buy me!" Perhaps it's skeptical voices we hear: "How can you believe that old stuff?

You've got to be kidding!" It could be the little cartoon devil on our shoulders, tempting us to disobey: "C'mon, everybody's doing it! It's nothing *too* bad." Very likely, it's all of the above. Too many voices from every angle, night and day, fill our minds with so much clutter that the voice of God simply gets drowned out by the static.

Faith comes through what is heard, scripture tells us. That's why it's important to make the extra effort, and create space to listen so that the voice which speaks most to our heart is the voice of the One who loves us the most.

ACT

I will spend ten minutes today in silent, wordless prayer (ie, no reading) and consider scheduling this kind of prayer on a regular basis, perhaps weekly if daily seems too much.

PRAY

Gentle God, teach me to create quiet time in my life just to rest in you. Amen.

Sunday, Fifth Week

BEGIN

Spend a minute or two in silence. Set aside whatever might hinder your prayer.

PRAY

Even now, says the Lord,
return to me with your whole heart;
for I am gracious and merciful.

~Joel 2:12–13

LISTEN

Read John 8:1–11

But when they continued asking him, Jesus straightened up and said to them, "Let the one among you who is without sin be the first to throw a stone at her." Again he bent down and wrote on the ground. And in response, they went away one by one, beginning with the elders. So he was left alone with the woman before him.

~John 8:7–9

Time to Think

In his lengthy poem about St. Joan of Arc, the French writer Charles Peguy intentionally left the first several pages blank. He did this, he explained, in order to give the reader time to think.

Perhaps giving people time to think is Jesus' motivation in today's gospel. Hostile men confront him about what to do with a woman who has been caught in adultery. But Jesus doesn't respond to them right away. Instead, he sits quietly on the ground, head bowed down, tracing his fingers in the dirt. It is only after the angry mob continues to press him for an answer that Jesus finally speaks. "Let the man among you who has no sin be the first to cast a stone." Upon hearing these words, the accusers drop the stones they intended to throw and slink away.

But why does Jesus take so long to speak? Why the hesitation? Is Jesus stalling for time so he can find something appropriate to say? Is he trying to figure out what to do in the midst of a tense, life-and-death situation? I don't think so.

It could be that Jesus is trying to teach them, and us, that we need to take the time to think before we impulsively cast a stone at another. We need to allow time for our emotions to cool so that our fear, anger, or prejudices don't get the best of us. We need time to consider all the variables and circumstances involved and to recall our own mistakes, shortcomings, and sins. Most of all, we need time to recall the abundant mercy God has shown us and asks that we show toward others.

ACT

I will pay attention to news headlines today and to my responses to them. What informs or guides my responses? Are they generated by my fear, anger, or prejudices? Or by God's tender mercy?

PRAY

Merciful God, heal my family, neighborhood, city, and nation of the wounds caused by bigotry and hatred. Help me be a sign of a different way to deal with conflict and divisions. Let me be a sign of your mercy. Amen.

Monday, Fifth Week

BEGIN

Spend a minute or two in silence. Set aside whatever might hinder your prayer.

PRAY

I take no pleasure in the death of the wicked man, says the Lord, but rather in his conversion, that he may live.

~Ezekiel 33:11

LISTEN

Read John 8:1–11

Then Jesus straightened up and said to her, "Woman, where are they? Has no one condemned you?" She replied, "No one, sir." Then Jesus said, "Neither do I condemn you. Go, [and] from now on do not sin any more."

~John 8:10–11

Reason to Rejoice

Children making their first confessions often struggle with the Act of Contrition. That's why when one girl offered it flawlessly, I congratulated her for a good job. But when I raised my hand for the prayer of absolution, she thought I was giving her a "high five," and she slapped my hand. All I could do was smile!

High fives are not in the Confession rite, but it's not inappropriate, because our encounter with God's mercy in that sacrament is certainly a cause for celebration! It's God who leads us to confess in the first place; it's God who fills us with the desire to unload our burdens; and it is God who wipes away our sins and pulls us close to him again, after our sins pulled us apart. Why shouldn't we rejoice?

However, sometimes we may approach confession not as an encounter with a living God, but as a "stay of execution" from a strict God of justice. We may feel like the woman in today's gospel—terrified by the threat of being stoned. But when she stood alone with Jesus, how relieved and joyful she must have felt that Jesus met her fear with kindness. In reconciliation, Jesus meets us with kindness too. The words he said to her, he says also to us: "Neither do I condemn you. Go, and sin no more."

ACT

I will check my parish website or bulletin for Confession times and arrange my schedule so that I can go before Easter.

If you haven't been for some time, the priest will help you, or you can search online for help on how to approach the sacrament.

PRAY

Lord Jesus Christ, may I always remember the sweetness of your mercy and rejoice in the freedom of your forgiveness. Amen.

Tuesday, Fifth Week

BEGIN

Spend a minute or two in silence. Set aside whatever might hinder your prayer.

PRAY

The seed is the word of God, Christ is the sower; all who come to him will live forever.

LISTEN

Read John 8:21–30

So Jesus said to them, "When you lift up the Son of Man, then you will realize that I AM."

~John 8:28

Understanding Jesus

Chrissie and her son Kevin were two individuals I came to know while in seminary. Chrissie had once been a nurse and Kevin an aspiring soccer player. But Chrissie became an alcoholic, and Kevin followed suit. They became homeless, roaming the streets, shouting obscenities, getting into fights, and regularly passing out on the sidewalk.

When praying one night, I shook my fist at God, demanding to know why he allowed this to happen. God answered by impressing upon my mind an image of the cross. I felt chastised but peaceful, because I'd been reminded of an essential truth: To know God, we need to know the cross; without the cross, we can't really understand God who entered our broken world to redeem it.

Jesus says as much in today's gospel. When asked, "Who are you?" Jesus explains that we will know that he is the Son of God when he is lifted up—lifted up on the cross.

To see Jesus on the cross is to understand who Jesus really is. On the cross, we see humility, obedience, suffering, mercy, forgiveness, glory, kingship, sacrifice, priesthood, death, and victory *over* death. But most importantly, we see love, because when Jesus was lifted up, he stretched out his arms as if to welcome us into the eternal embrace of his love. Truly, to know the cross is to know Jesus. And to know Jesus is to experience his love.

ACT

I will name the crosses I bear in my life right now. How is it that I find God through them?

PRAY

Christ crucified, help me to comprehend something of your death on the cross and the glory of your resurrection. Teach me to pattern my life after this holy mystery; continually accepting the many deaths life brings in order to find new life in you. Amen.

WEDNESDAY, FIFTH WEEK

BEGIN

Spend a minute or two in silence. Set aside whatever might hinder your prayer.

PRAY

Blessed are they who have kept the word with a generous heart and yield a harvest through perseverance.

~Luke 8:15

LISTEN

Read John 8:31–42

Jesus said to those Jews who believed in him, "If you remain in my word, you will truly be my disciples, and you will know the truth, and the truth will set you free."

~John 8:31–32

Free to Do What's Right

"I'm free to do what I want, any old time!" insist the Rolling Stones. Their classic song "I'm Free" reflects how so many people today understand freedom: doing whatever we want, whenever we want to.

On the other hand, Jesus speaks in today's gospel of a freedom not to do as we please, but the freedom to do what is pleasing to God. He speaks of a freedom that involves not just the right to make choices, but the freedom to choose what is right; not a freedom from discipline, but a freedom dependent on discipline; a freedom that doesn't give us a license to sin, but a freedom that liberates us from sin; a freedom not just to "be you and me," but a freedom to become all we are meant to be.

This freedom is rooted in knowledge of a truth that is not just a body of knowledge, but is a person—Jesus Christ our Lord. What Jesus is saying to us today, then, is that if we follow him and live as he taught, we will truly be free *from* sin, distress, and fear, and free *to* love, to be his brothers and sisters, and sons and daughters of God.

ACT

I will contemplate what I understand freedom to be and consider whether my experience is truly rooted in following Jesus.

PRAY

Lord Jesus Christ, free my heart and my mind to follow you today and every day. Amen.

Thursday, Fifth Week

Suffering Like Jesus

On more than one occasion, Jesus found himself in grave danger. As a newborn, Herod's soldiers threatened him. A mob hostile to his preaching once tried to throw him off a cliff. And in today's gospel, he faces a stone-wielding crowd. But on all of these occasions, Jesus escaped from the violence.

That's good for us to reflect on. Sometimes we think that as a follower of Jesus we need to accept and absorb whatever suffering may come our way—be it verbal, physical, or both. We recall Jesus' words that we should turn the other cheek when struck, and that all who follow him should expect to carry a cross, just as he did.

But Jesus suffered only when it was necessary so that he might fulfill the Father's will for his life. We'll also likely encounter suffering at various times in our lives as we try to follow God's will. But there was other suffering Jesus faced that he avoided on purpose—suffering that would simply have made him a victim of others' illness, ignorance, or sin, such as with spousal abuse for us.

To follow Jesus isn't to become a doormat or a punching bag. Suffering will indeed come our way. Some of it we're meant to embrace, that we might become more like Jesus. But some, as Jesus himself shows us, we will do best to avoid.

ACT

I will pray today for people throughout the world who are persecuted because of their faith. And I will pray for those who do the persecuting.

PRAY

Redeeming God, Jesus died on the cross because he boldly preached the truth. Give me the courage to do your will by announcing the coming of your kingdom in what I speak and what I do. Amen.

FRIDAY, FIFTH WEEK

BEGIN

Spend a minute or two in silence. Set aside whatever might hinder your prayer.

PRAY

Your words, Lord, are Spirit and life;
you have the words of everlasting life.

~John 6:63c, 68c

LISTEN

Read John 10:31–42

The Jews picked up rocks to stone Jesus. Jesus answered them, "I have shown you many good works from my Father. For which of these are you trying to stone me?" The Jews answered him, "We are not stoning you for a good work but for blasphemy. You, a man, are making yourself God."

~John 10:31–33

Pots Calling Kettles Black

"The pot calling the kettle black" is how we describe a person who is guilty of the very thing of which they accuse another. We encounter a classic case in today's gospel when certain critics scold Jesus, saying, "You, a man, are making yourself God!"

Of course, Jesus isn't *making* himself God—he *is* God! However, don't we try to make ourselves God all the time? Isn't this an accusation that Jesus could legitimately make of his accusers and many others, including us?

Just think about it: So often, we want to glorify ourselves, and not God; we want to be independent, not dependent on God; we want to do what we want, not what God wants; we want God to serve us, not the other way around.

The truth is that God didn't create us to be God. God created us to be ourselves. That is a very good thing, as we're all made in God's image and likeness. And that's why God calls us, not to *be* God, but to be godly, God-like.

Our challenge, then, is for us to stop trying so hard to be God, and instead surrender to God. Only that way will we become like God, just a little bit more, every day.

ACT

I will practice *not* trying to control everything and not seeing myself as the chief engineer of my life. I will instead try to accept this day as total gift and rejoice in it.

PRAY

Father Almighty, you have created all good things, including me. Open my heart to your majesty and teach me to reflect your image to my world. Amen.

SATURDAY, FIFTH WEEK

BEGIN

Spend a minute or two in silence. Set aside whatever might hinder your prayer.

PRAY

Cast away from you all the crimes you have committed, says the Lord, and make for yourselves a new heart and a new spirit.

~Ezekiel 18:31

LISTEN

Read John 11:45–56

Many of the Jews who had come to Mary and seen what Jesus had done began to believe in him. But some of them went to the Pharisees and told them what Jesus had done.

~John 11:45–46

Should We Stay or Go?

"Should I stay or go?" is what Jesus asks of all those who encounter him. In today's gospel, we're reminded that this question can give rise to a variety of responses. After having "seen what Jesus had done," some begin to believe in him. Others, however, report him to the Jewish authorities.

How do we answer when Jesus asks, "Should I stay or go?" How do we react when we encounter him? Chances are, it depends. Sometimes we leap for joy; sometimes we turn our head the other way; sometimes we run like crazy.

When we ignore or avoid Jesus, it's likely we're afraid that he'll take us out of our comfort zones. We fear that he might ask us to change, or that following him might be inconvenient, embarrassing, or even dangerous. Like Caiaphas, we might conclude that eliminating Jesus will help keep the peace. But excluding Jesus from our lives, or even a part of our lives, will never bring us peace.

True peace can only come through welcoming Jesus and allowing him to remain with us. That's why when he asks us, "Should I stay or go?" we can be assured that Jesus never, ever, wishes to be sent away.

ACT

I will question my heart to see if there are places here where I do not welcome the Lord. If there are, I will try to create a plan to break the habit of keeping him out.

PRAY

Lord Jesus, I fling wide the doors of my heart so that you may enter there. Amen.

Passion (Palm) Sunday

BEGIN

Spend a minute or two in silence. Set aside whatever might hinder your prayer.

PRAY

Christ became obedient to the point of death, even death on a cross. Because of this, God greatly exalted him and bestowed on him the name which is above every name.

~Philippians 2:8–9

LISTEN

Read Luke 22:14—23:56 (or shorter: 23:1–49)

After withdrawing about a stone's throw from them and kneeling, Jesus prayed, saying, "Father, if you are willing, take this cup away from me; still, not my will but yours be done." And to strengthen him an angel from heaven appeared to him. He was in such agony and he prayed so fervently that his sweat became like drops of blood falling on the ground. When he rose from prayer and returned to his disciples, he found them sleeping from grief. He said to them, "Why are you sleeping? Get up and pray that you may not undergo the test."

~Luke 22:41–46

Beyond Our Fears

Life can be frightening at times. In the Garden of Gethsemane, Jesus and his sleepy disciples were all understandably afraid. But they reacted to the same fearful situation in very different ways. At least one disciple lashed out in violence, and all of them ran away, leaving their friend and teacher to those who hated him. For his part, Jesus was probably angry, but certainly not violent; he was afraid, but courageous too. His fortitude was greater than his fear.

Why this difference? To begin with, Jesus trusted in God his Father. Through this trust, Jesus knew that evil and darkness would not have the final word, and that the Father would always be with him, even in his darkest hours. Jesus was assured that beyond the sufferings he would endure, there was something better for him, and something better for the rest of us, too.

Prayer fed this trust and assurance of Jesus. In Gethsemane, the disciples failed to pray, even after Jesus had essentially ordered them to. That's one reason why, when the test came, they failed and fled the scene. On the other hand, Jesus prayed through his fears, and shared them with the Father: "Let this cup pass from me!" At the same time, he surrendered himself into the Father's hands, asking for help to do what the Father wanted him to do: "Nevertheless, not as I will, but what you will."

In imitation of Jesus, we need not let our fears defeat us. Whenever frightened, we too can turn to our heavenly Father in prayer, and find in him all the hope and courage we need.

ACT

I will consider today my greatest fears. Am I truly willing to let God be with me as I face them?

PRAY

Father, as Holy Week begins, let me be focused on the sacred days that lie ahead. I place my trust in you. Amen.

MONDAY OF HOLY WEEK

BEGIN

Spend a minute or two in silence. Set aside whatever might hinder your prayer.

PRAY

Hail to you, our King;
you alone are compassionate with our faults.

LISTEN

Read John 12:1–11

Six days before Passover Jesus came to Bethany, where Lazarus was, whom Jesus had raised from the dead. They gave a dinner for him there, and Martha served, while Lazarus was one of those reclining at table with him. Mary took a liter of costly perfumed oil made from genuine aromatic nard and anointed the feet of Jesus and dried them with her hair.

~John 12:1–3a

Friendship with Jesus

Mary and Martha were close friends of Jesus'. We may recall the story of Jesus raising their brother Lazarus from the dead. Another time, during a meal together, Martha complained that Mary sat listening to Jesus speak while she was busy serving. Jesus had to gently explain to her that, on this occasion, Mary had made the better choice.

Today's gospel finds Martha serving once again, while Mary worships Jesus by anointing his feet with oil. We who also wish to be friends of Jesus should look closely at Mary's and Martha's examples. Martha shows us that friends of Jesus are servants. They serve their Lord and one other, especially the poor. Mary's witness reminds us of the importance of prayer and worship. You and I would do well to combine the virtues of Mary and Martha and nourish our friendship with Jesus through prayer, worship, and service.

Both of these elements are necessary. Prayer and worship without service can become hollow flattery. Service without prayer and worship can become misguided, self-serving, or lead to burn out. Just consider Mother Teresa. Without question, she was one of God's great servants and certainly a friend of Jesus. She accomplished amazing things in her life. How? "My secret is simple," she confessed. "I pray."

ACT

I will find a way to serve Christ present in the poor. Many people are in profound need that is not necessarily economic, yet they too need my help.

PRAY

Lord, let me not neglect my prayer life for the sake of doing good. And let me not neglect acts of mercy and of justice in order to have more time for prayer Amen.

TUESDAY OF HOLY WEEK

BEGIN

Spend a minute or two in silence. Set aside whatever might hinder your prayer.

PRAY

Hail to you, our King, obedient to the Father; you were led to your crucifixion like a gentle lamb to the slaughter.

LISTEN

Read John 13:21–33, 36–38

When he had left, Jesus said,
"Now is the Son of Man glorified, and God is glorified in him. If God is glorified in him, God will also glorify him in himself, and he will glorify him at once.
My children, I will be with you only a little while longer. You will look for me, and as I told the Jews, 'Where I go you cannot come,' so now I say it to you."

~John 13:31–33

Stopping at Nothing

"Neither snow nor rain nor gloom of night," tradition claims, will keep US mail carriers from completing their rounds. To complete his mission of redemption and salvation, Jesus had to contend with much worse than that, as today's gospel reminds us. Darkness, denial, ignorance, betrayal, cowardice, and the demonic all confront Jesus at the Last Supper, on the eve of his Passion. Yet Jesus presses on, in spite of it all, demonstrating that his love for us, and his desire to save us, will never fail.

Jesus' love is resolute. He would never force himself upon us, but he doesn't keep a polite distance either. Instead, he keeps knocking at the door of our hearts. Sometimes we open our hearts to him on our own and welcome him in. At other times, we need his help. Maybe our hearts are frozen, and Jesus needs to melt them; it could be that our hearts are broken, and Jesus needs to mend them; perhaps our hearts are made of stone, and they need to be replaced with the tender and sacred heart of Jesus.

Regardless of the state of our hearts, Jesus persists in his efforts to open their doors, not to assert his power but to share his love. Nothing will stop him! Not even death itself.

ACT

I will listen throughout the day for Jesus knocking on the door of my heart. I will open the door to him by my loving response to all whom I encounter.

PRAY

Tender and Sacred Heart of Jesus, change my heart to be more like yours. Amen.

WEDNESDAY OF HOLY WEEK

BEGIN

Spend a minute or two in silence. Set aside whatever might hinder your prayer.

PRAY

Hail to you, our King;
you alone are compassionate with our errors.

LISTEN

Read Matthew 26:14–25

When it was evening, he reclined at table with
the Twelve. And while they were eating, he said,
"Amen, I say to you, one of you will betray me."
Then Judas, his betrayer, said in reply, "Surely it is
not I, Rabbi?" He answered, "You have said so."

~Matthew 26:20–21, 25

No Need to Despair

What is it that motivates Judas to betray Jesus? Is
he trying to force Jesus to display his divine powers
against his enemies? Maybe he is resentful that he
wasn't chosen as leader of the apostles. Or perhaps
he is simply malicious and greedy. We just don't know.
What we do know from later in Matthew's gospel is
that in the end Judas is overwhelmed by bitter regret.
He tries to return his blood money and ends his life
in suicide.

Suicide is always a tragedy. But the greater tragedy
here is that Judas loses hope. In his despair, Judas loses
hope of receiving mercy from the one whose entire life
conveyed hope and mercy. We can say with absolute

confidence that if Judas had run to the foot of the cross and begged forgiveness, he would have received it.

In a way, Judas represents the state of many people today—people who live lives of quiet despair, shame, and fear because they believe themselves to be unlovable and unforgivable in the eyes of God. But such fear is a self-inflicted wound. The good news of Holy Week is that no one should despair of God's mercy and forgiveness. Not Judas Iscariot. Not you or me.

ACT

I will examine my life and try to answer truthfully whether or not I trust completely God's promise of forgiveness. If I find sins in need of mercy, I will take these to the Lord in prayer and if possible to the Sacrament of Penance.

PRAY

Lord Jesus Christ, have mercy on me, a sinner. Heal my broken heart and set me free. Amen.

HOLY THURSDAY

BEGIN

Spend a minute or two in silence. Set aside whatever might hinder your prayer.

PRAY

I give you a new commandment, says the Lord:
love one another as I have loved you.

~John 13:34

LISTEN

Read John 13:1–15

If I, therefore, the master and teacher, have washed
your feet, you ought to wash one another's feet.
I have given you a model to follow, so that as I have
done for you, you should also do.

~John 13:14–15

A Model of Service

There they sit in silence, their feet caked with mud. Not
one of Jesus' disciples makes a move to wash the others' feet. Foot washing was expected, but was normally
done only by those of the lowest social standing. How
shocked they are when Jesus does the job himself. He
does this to give them, and to give us, an example of
humble service and to announce the radical nature of
life in the kingdom of God. He in fact seems to turn
certain expectations about proper order upside down.

The service to which Jesus calls us is both generous and selfless. It's motivated, first and foremost, by
a sincere concern for the well being of others. It isn't
driven by a desire for recognition or reward; it doesn't
demand gratitude or payback from those we serve,

and it's not focused upon trying to feel good about ourselves.

That's a high standard, to be sure, and very often we fall short. Our motives when serving are usually mixed, even on our best days. So often we want to *do* good and *look* good, all at the same time. But Jesus understands this. Maybe that's why he made his call to service within the context of the Last Supper—the sacred meal at which he instituted the Holy Eucharist.

At every Eucharist, you and I are joined to Jesus' sacrifice, the most selfless act of loving service in history. Through our union with this act, Jesus works to liberate our acts of service from the desire for self-promotion and self-gratification. Understood this way, Jesus' words "do this in memory of me" take on a new meaning. Not only do they command us to take and to receive, but they also direct us to give and to share.

ACT

I will find at least one opportunity to turn expectations upside down by raising up those who are otherwise pushed to the margins or considered insignificant.

PRAY

Lord, help me to serve your people on bended knee with a humble and tender heart. Amen.

GOOD FRIDAY

BEGIN

Spend a minute or two in silence. Set aside whatever might hinder your prayer.

PRAY

Christ became obedient to the point of death,
even death on a cross. Because of this, God greatly
exalted him and bestowed on him the name which
is above every other name.

~*Philippians 2:8–9*

LISTEN

Read John 18:1–19:42

After this, aware that everything was now finished,
in order that the Scripture might be fulfilled,
Jesus said, "I thirst." There was a vessel filled
with common wine. So they put a sponge soaked
in wine on a sprig of hyssop and put it up to his
mouth. When Jesus had taken the wine, he said,
"It is finished." And bowing his head, he handed
over the spirit.

~*John 19:28–30*

How Much Are We Worth

How much is one human life worth? Is it the combined
value of the chemicals and minerals in our body? If
so, then the typical human life is worth less than one
dollar. Or perhaps it is one's possessions that determine a life's worth. But if that's the case, then the life
of someone like Mother Teresa was almost worthless.
What our lives are worth to God shines through clearly
in today's Passion narrative.

God considers us so valuable that his only Son surrendered his own life so that we might live forever. If God thought that we were cheap, expendable, or a dime a dozen, he wouldn't have bothered. But through the suffering and death of Jesus, we know how precious we are in the sight of God.

Judas Iscariot received thirty silver pieces for Jesus' life. But that was an intentional insult, as it represented the fine for injuring a slave. Joseph of Arimathea and Nicodemus anointed Jesus' dead body with over a hundred pounds of costly spices, an extravagant amount fit only for a king. Yet even this comes nowhere near to representing the true value of Jesus' life. The life of Jesus is priceless. And if Jesus' life is priceless, then the same is true of ours.

The cross shows us, more than anything else, how profoundly we are cherished and loved by God. We may not be able to place a dollar value on our lives, but thanks to the Cross, you and I know *exactly* what our lives are worth.

ACT

As I contemplate the Cross at church or at home, I will consider what I am doing with this precious, priceless life God has given me. Am I living it fully, doing God's will, and being ever grateful?

PRAY

Precious Lord, you died upon the Cross for my sake and the sake of all the world. By emptying yourself—your entire self—you broke the power of sin and death. Help me to embrace your Cross and so experience eternal life. Amen.

R. Scott Hurd serves as vicar general for the Personal Ordinariate of the Chair of St. Peter. A priest of the Archdiocese of Washington, he is former executive director of the Archdiocesan Office of the Permanent Diaconate, and has also served in the Archdiocesan Office for Religious Education. Hurd began his professional ministry as an Episcopal priest, entered the Catholic Church in 1996, and was ordained a Catholic priest four years later. He and his wife live with their three school-aged children in Alexandria, Virginia. Hurd's first book, *Forgiveness: A Catholic Approach*, was published in 2011. Follow Hurd online at fatherscotthurd. blogspot.com.